C000177212

Gathering Light

A Cramond Causeway

David Bleiman

For Maureen, who gathers the light

Gathering Light
© David Bleiman

First Edition 2022

David Bleiman has asserted his authorship and given permission
to Dempsey & Windle for these poems to be published here.

All rights reserved. No part of this publication may be
reproduced, stored in a retrieval system or transmitted in any
form or by any means without the written consent of the author,
nor otherwise circulated in any form of binding or cover other
than that in which it is published and without a similar condition
being imposed on a subsequent purchaser.

Published by Dempsey & Windle

15 Rosetrees
Guildford
Surrey
GU1 2HS
UK
01483 571164
dempseyandwindle.com

A catalogue record for this book is available from the British
Library

British Library Cataloguing-in-Publication Data

ISBN: 978-1-913329-68-6

Printed and bound in the UK

Foreword

Cramond is certainly worth a poem. During a global pandemic we have the opportunity to appreciate perceptive thoughts expressed through penetrating language by someone who resides in our midst. These poems invite reflection; by doing this you will discover a poet bringing new insights on Cramond and far beyond.

The Heron's Dream (p.28) was a winning entry in the *Imagine Cramond* competition and David's profits from this booklet will go to *Cramond Commemorates*, a tree and bulb planting project to mark the losses of the Covid era. David attended when children from our local schools planted the first oak. *We Plant Poetry* (p.17) is a poem compiled from the words of pupils of Cramond Primary School who shared their own poems on that sunny day.

Poems endure and can speak to us over generations. TS Eliot's masterpiece, *The Four Quartets,* started in real places, like East Coker, Somerset during a global upheaval, the Second World War. These *Quartets* are still read, and during lockdown the actor Ralph Fiennes memorised them and is taking them into theatres.

If you thirst for more, David has another booklet, *This Kilt of Many Colours.*

I commend this booklet to you and ask that you read it and discover a new take on an old community.

Reverend Ian Gilmour (Locum Minister, Cramond Kirk)

Contents

Gathering Light

This was the day we went out
to collect the light,
took poles, fitted grippers,
stepped onto the ice.

Our first catch was a shiver,
glinting off the river ripples,
tickling the neck of the eider,
flicking the edge of the shore.

A mozzarella moon
made a creamy face in the pines
and as the sun peered in
shimmered down to a see-through sliver.

Soon we were slipping on sunlight
that slid off the ice on the foreshore,
bleaching the cotton Ochils
over the snowfields of Fife.

When it came blinding over the estuary,
sun skimming an unruffled sea,
we gloved our eyes, blinked up
and the moon was away.

This is the day we catch the dusk,
lipstick kissing cloudy collars,
twilight dapples in the gloaming,
gilds this glass that warms the night.

Elusive Edges

At low tide
        one
        can
        cross/
        cross
        the
            causeway
                to the island/
                    not an island.

Leaving aside tides and tables,
to isolate, lose and forget oneself,
to walk on the waters,
where the line between sand and sea is fudged,
when the line between sea and sky is fuddled.

We always had a liquid borderline,
Romans from the south,
Picts to the north,
a powerful empire
and those wild tribes.

The tide rises and falls,
falls and rises,
we remain,
not knowing if we live in a village or a city,
an island or a peninsula.

Our kirk just a pile of Roman stones,
remains
of the frontier fort.
Is God one, three or many?
Maybe none.

These tattooed strangers,
are they natives or tourists,
Picts or Italians?
We don't know–
we live beside the river

in the dirty mouth
of the estuary,
in country
or city,
in village or suburb.

Are we in Cramond or Edinburgh,
Edinburgh or Scotland,
Scotland or Britain,
Britain or Europe?
We don't know

and I fear this uncertainty
on the muddy margin between past and future,
between ourselves and others,
this border between you and me,
my enemy, my lover.

And if one were able to breach the border?
If I could have crossed that marshy membrane
between head and heart,
my mind would have followed
the cloudy currents of my soul.

The Village on Cramond Island

A poster at Spoons in Corstorphine
portrays a village on the island,
accessible at low tide. Have tourists,
trippers, walked the long causeway,
looking for that offshore village?
No, here we are still on the mainland:
isolated, insular
but not islanded,
though the authorities try
and try again to make it so.
When they closed the Post Office,
the corner shop followed;
our bus belongs to other places,
zigzagging through the suburbs,
seeking out roadworks and traffic jams,
diversions and delays,
landing exhausted at the end of time.
Only when the traffic's tide is low,
when the rain is off,
when our legs are strong,
do we stride across to the mainland,
from our lost urban village of the seas.

Contact

*One light-year equals **5,878,625,370,000 miles** (9.5 trillion km)*

If it comes
it won't be little green men,
take me to your leader,
come up to my saucer sometime.

If it ever comes
it won't be a conversation,
you are breaking up,
log off and try again.

If it comes at all
it won't be your letter just arrived,
you forgot the stamp,
the post is not what it was.

It won't even come
like a Christmas card comes
to a friend who died five years ago
and forgot to say.

It may be a ring of stones,
a setting sun
at the equinox
asking a question:

Is anyone still there?
We were here when the light left
and we looked at the stars
just like you.

Diaspora Dream

So rooted here, I am become a tree,
washed in on flames of choice the wind has fanned,
like all the others looking out to sea.

Though not a son of this community,
I grow around your railings, here I stand,
so rooted here, I am become a tree.

Another stripe in your geology,
a layer in the rock, a sandstone band,
like all the others looking back to sea.

A fine example, 1953–
you count my rings and try to understand
why, rooted here, I am become a tree.

I am grown tall and tied, yet landing free,
your breeze/my branches shape a wishing sound,
like all the others looking out to sea.

And in this dream you make a bench of me,
to sit, while children dabble in the sand,
so rooted here, I am become a tree,
like all the others looking out to sea.

Cramond Island
for Ronald Rae, FRSS

Walk out to the island,
  not for the island itself,
ghosts of gun emplacements
    and graffiti,
   go only for the hillock
  of a suburban island,
    only to look back,
     to see the world
        small
       as it is.

Walk back by the Kirk,
  not for the kirk itself,
  ruins of Roman baths
     and repentance,
  go behind the car park,
       granite
   on the grassy verge,
  Ronnie is carving again,
        striking
through grief and arthritis,
thirty years after that weary promise:
 "I've carved my last stone",
    hitting the granite,
        hard
       as it is.

[13]

Faraway Cottages Revisited

(Fair-a-Far, Gaelic, ridge of the cultivated ground)

Faraway Cottages he called them,
on that last, long walk before the embolism,
as we took arm in arm down Whitehouse Road,
where the workers were housed by Fair-a-Far mill.

It was a glorious day,
his disposition was also sunny
and, taking his arm,
I felt a warmth,
from me or from him, no matter,
I was, at last, grown up,
enjoying this man who made me,
without reserve or reservations.

So was it just a joke,
like when he died on stage,
later, laughing,
at his lecture in Nottingham?

It *was* him and he *was* far away
from London and Cape Town
and the cares of an erratic life,
strolling slowly towards the gallery,
to sit in the winter sun
and look out on the gulls
and the tide
going out of the Almond.

Not Seeing the Wood for the Words

I feel the sting of rain–
I would ungain this art of speech,
be animal again,
cold, wet and hungry,
smelling the air,
wanting a piss to scent a bush.

But we are clouds
in borrowed trousers
and what feels raw and real
is only what was sown aloud
to grow.

So, wandering lonely through these words,
we forest bathe our minds
in leaf alliteration,
pervading place with metaphor
and fool the cultured brain to claim
that nature oozes images in rhyme.

This walk's a poet's holiday,
we beat a meter in the mud,
down to the roosting place of rooks
and eddies in the river's tongue,
where lockdown-quiffed goosanders dip,
sweet chestnut in the winter sun

and promise,
if we come again in June,
a crush of fuzzy chicks will hop
on mother's back–
like us–
to hitch a ride
where words run out
of wild.

End of Term

Down School Brae again,
a chill wind funnels
up the river Almond
as dark waves shadow-dash
the schoolhouse wall.

We all chase shades of infants,
playing on the wall
and trace these chimes of childhood,
fading in or out of earshot,
happy on the wind.

Might there be more at Cockle Mill?
A grandchild's poem thrown into the pond,
this plashing pebble breaking light,
may sound my silhouette
against a distant ground.

We Plant Poetry

On 4 November 2021, the children of class P4, Cramond Primary
School helped plant a tree for 'Cramond Commemorates'. This
poem is made from their own words.

When we are old– I'm guessing thirty-three–
I'll take you back and we can see
what's happened to the tree
we plant today for Cramond.

Trees grow like humans, step by step,
their branches stretching far and wide,
soft leaves, like feathers, floating in the air,
reach out, soaking up the sun.

I like it when it's gloomy,
you like me when it's sunny,
come under, share my shade,
join all the animals living in me!

Tall as the clouds
and every root is an emotion,
my seed drops down,
my spirit radiates as I rise.

That's why we plant a tree and write our poetry,
a tree will reach out like a friend,
with love and hope for all the world,
our spirit radiates as we rise.

Fair-a-Far Fish Ladder
(Fair-a-Far Fish Pass officially opened in April 2018)

She was the one who wrote *a woman needs a man,*
not Gloria Steinem but Irina Patsi Dunn,
on the door of the loo in Woolloomooloo
the etymology of the place remains obscure,
referencing, some say, a young black kangaroo,
but I digress. Ms Dunn picked up her pen
or marker–history is silent on the implement
and, fifty years on, the trail's gone cold–
continued, *like a fish,* you see where this is going,
needs (I hope she washed her hands) *a bicycle.*

Gathered at this River Almond Walkway, friends,
I see you wondering where this story ends,
I only know where it began, down at the weir,
at Fair-a-Far, when I found out that fish,
well...
fish need a ladder, like a woman needs,
well...
someone or something–
it's not for man to specify–
to leap life's rapids.

February Flashback

When earth has drained its fill
and rain, rebuffed, clings to
the claggy furrows of the brae

when half the road's a pool
that swamps the leaf-clogged stank

pert potholes cup the murky slosh
wink saucily at lorries gushing by
waking the weary bus queue in their drench

winter's wet eyes lash up and catch
unlooked-for shafts of Scotland
braw and bright
these fleeting breaches of the dreich

flaming the creamy underside of clouds

igniting flashy gulls
to dance the storm.

Unoaked

Come away from the window, come for tea.
They took our oak down. Comfort me.

Innocent of ill intent, our great oak shaded
Mrs Rankin's renowned Refreshment Rooms,
where peak-capped boys
watched carriages from Barnton Station
take Sunday outings to Cramond beach,
posted us piles of leafmail every Autumn,
lodged Nordic waxwings through that winter.

Do you remember the waxwings?
I saw a white squirrel in the snow that winter.
Do you believe me?

At the window, car doors slam for school.
I watch the saplings, wondering
what trace is left by shadow of oak leaves
on a tea room's sandstone wall
in an Edwardian postcard?
How do the branches sway
in an unrecorded breeze?

Why are those ragged boys
leaning over the wall?
Stamped and postmarked 1905–
the tree was all we still could touch.

And now that it is gone?
There will be an *Acorn Nursery,*
there will be an *Oak View Nursing Home.*

With time, with reckless negligence,
a tree *is* capable of crime,
whipping the windows on the upper deck,
working the wind to crunch a car
and break a limb,
a tree is capable of manslaughter.

The Council's law is arm for arm
and our oak now joins, half its height,
an olden grove of beggar stumps
fit only for a dog to lift a leg:
unlimbed, unleaving and unboughed.

Vicarious Fall

after W.H.Auden's 'Musée des Beaux Arts'

The chop-chop-chopping of the air
tugged us down river
and as the estuary stuck its tongue
to the island
we saw a rescue helicopter hovering
almost motionless
above an empty sea
in which nothing was happening.

Families eating ice cream
on cheap folding chairs
got up to blink at the sky,
someone was opening a window,
the professional dog walkers
took their doggy packs
to the edge of the sandbank
to listen out for a splash.

The coastguard and two ambulances,
half of the city taking a walk,
but everyone stopped to stare,
and when it turned out
to have been an exercise
there was a little disappointment.
They understood none of this,
the Old Masters.

Unaccountable

Countless, these joys –
sunshine, fresh air and, yes, the rain–
yet countable
flat cans
line the path,
card cups
sticky with fizz,
still poke their straws,
scooped poop
hangs in bags
arranged on railings,
gloves and socks–
always singletons,
never in pairs–
but here a pair of peachy knickers,
singular,
meets a milky moon
in the pooling drain.

Who dropped these drawers
and why,
going down School Brae,
halfway to the strand,
where a solitary stand
of Scots pine
grips the estuary edge
of unfathomable sky?

Confinement Quartet

(I) Wuhan, 27 January 2020

" *Wuhan jiayóu!* Add oil!"
from a window high up there;
I am stuck in my flat in the Year of the Rat,
stocked with dumplings, rice, salted eggs–
and I don't even like salted eggs.
Someone starts to sing, lights flash
from block to block across that empty night;
we know where it started,
don't know when it ends
but someone sings *Dear Motherland*
and people over here join in
and so it goes viral.

(II) Rome, 13 March 2020

I don't have a flag or much of a voice
just some pot lids to ring out a din;
a boy leans over his balcony rail
and strums a guitar in a lazy way,
smiles, as if he knows me;
two schoolgirls hold up a cardboard sign–
andra tutto bene– yes, all will be well;
a tenor I have never met
sings *Nessun Dorma,* no one sleeps,
and now someone is singing *Volare*
and people in another flat join in
and I hear myself sing.

(III) Madrid, 14 March 2020

We all agreed to applaud them–
our nurses, doctors and carers–
on the hour at ten o'clock;
I am shut in my flat with an exercise mat
which I'll lay on the floor
where the sun strikes at four
and pretend I am out in the park;
I wait at my window to join the applause
when Dad Skypes from Scotland
and hears all the clapping
and wonders what's up
until I join in.

(IV) Cramond, 16 March 2020

With pubs, theatres, social life closing,
my diary can go in the bin;
I will go for long walks in my head,
the pamphlets I stockpiled will all now be read;
I just got a few things from the store–
bulbs of garlic from China, a case of Chianti,
manchego from Spain, nothing more.
No one sings in the space of these suburbs,
too windy for balconies, too cold and wet;
my mouse will dance, my keyboard fly
across these clean and silent skies
and you'll join in.

Question Mark in the Sky

Black cat bounds
out of February night
and something above lights up as I crest the path.

This asterism, these seven distant lights,
an ancient movie, black and white,
still showing
on the big screen.

Still showing tonight is the starry plough,
the saucepan and cleaver,
the salmon net and a bucket of fish,
seven sons, their mother's stepping stones,
a coffin and three mourners,
the wall of the forbidden enclosure.

Some saw the magic medicine wagon
that cures all ills
and I need all those pills tonight,
looking up so long
that I'm up
looking down
on those who made these meanings

and a black cat
with a curious tail
curling up the night
to a question.

Peninsularity

On a blue day
such as this,
an ant rests
on the rim
of a bicycle tire
(the bike propped on its stand)
and sees only a muddy way
that streaks the sky.

On a clear night
such as this,
we stared out from the edge
and though we lay
all night
in the damp grass,
saw only spilled milk
running in a rut
through the peaty soil.

No, you can never see
the spinning wheel
spiralling alight
across the whole bright night,
you're watching from close up,
step back,
you need a better vantage.

From here.
Do you see it now?

The Heron's Dream

At the bus stop, perched on the edge of the pavement,
peering up the road like a heron,
patiently waiting in case of a forty-one,
there is time to dream and imagine...

Imagine buses leaping up Whitehouse Road,
the Almond full of salmon at the Grotto,
children's laughter bubbling on the Walkway
as we whizz by in wheelchairs skipping Salvesen Steps,
imagine having a steam like a Roman, in the baths
by the sports grounds on Cramond Road North,
imagine the new flightpath,
a sky sounding only of crows and of curlews,
smelling only of breeze and wild garlic,
grandchildren growing sturdy like plantings
of oak and of sycamore, stands of Scots pine,
imagine a shop we can walk to again,
for bread, milk and eggs and a place to post parcels,
to dawdle and ask after neighbours,
an absence of litter, it's hard to imagine the lack of it,
no crushed cans nor bottles, no cartons, no masks,
imagine visitors strolling down Glebe Road,
arm in arm, on the road,
no queues of cars churning engines, no diesel,
only a shuttle buzzing back and forth to the Forth,
imagine me too, as another bird, another species,
imagine me, maybe, as mother Goosander,
in the sparkling late Spring, down there by the steps
under the new footbridge to Dalmeny
and all my wee chicks hopping on and off for the ride...

Imagine all this in the heron's dream,
still waiting, patiently waiting
on Whitehouse Road for the chance of a 41,
waiting for a Council to thank for all this...

Imagine!

The Last Word in Alliteration

Is this collection
a cameo or a canvas?
Cabinet or casket?
Catchment or cataract?
Cadenza or cacophony?
Cappucino or cauldron?
Cabaret or cartwheel?
Cairn or catechism?

Cast loose and castaway,
Cramond calls me,
caressing and calmative,
and this–
another cobble
on a causeway.

Acknowledgements

'The Village on Cramond Island' was included in the Scottish Writers' Centre chapbook, 'City, Town & Village', 2020.

'Diaspora Dream' was commended in the Poetry Society's 2021 Stanza competition on the theme of 'Choice'.

'The Heron's Dream' was one of the winners in the 'Imagine Cramond' competition, 2021. It was published in 'The Grapevine' (Cramond Kirk Magazine), September 2021.

Thank you for 'We Plant Poetry', Class P4 of Cramond Primary, your teacher, Jay Cook, and your head teacher, Helen Donaldson.

*

I would like to thank...

I have the good fortune to belong to three local poetry workshops where some of these poems first showed face: the Edinburgh Stanza of the Poetry Society, the School of Poets and the 'Others'.

Cramond is my adoptive home (see 'Diaspora Dream'!) where my poetry has flourished in its endlessly fascinating natural and human environment. This pamphlet owes much to the enthusiasm of the Revd Ian Gilmour, locum Minister of Cramond Kirk and the support of Adam Cumming of the Cramond Association.

Special thanks to Anne Hay for her collaboration on a 'River of Verse' event for the Cramond Association in April 2021, where some of these poems were performed. If the 41 bus ever appoints a poet in residence, Anne and I will have to do it as a job-share.

If you've enjoyed these poems you might also enjoy

This Kilt of Many Colours
by David Bleiman

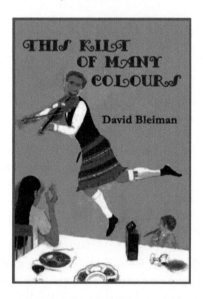

David Bleiman has captured perfectly the blend of his essential ingredients: dark brilliance and emotional intensity drawn from family history and the mixter maxter of his own journey.
— Jim Mackintosh, poet and editor

Bleiman displays his love of languages and humankind in poems which weave a fabric at once local and universal; persistently beautiful and bound to endure.
— John Glenday, poet

Published May 2021, RRP £8.00
Available from www.dempseyandwindle.com/davidbleiman